A Random Walk
Down Bull Street

(A Savannah Tour Guide)

John H. Maclean

Published 2019

Printed in the United States of America
Print ISBN: 978-1951490324

Canoe Tree Press
4697 Main Street
Manchester, VT 05255

www.CanoeTreePress.com

To my wife, Brigitte Maclean

Contents

Preface

This is a walking and history travelogue of Bull Street, the main road through old Savannah.

My family has been in and around Savannah since its beginning. Some of the family came to Charleston around 1685 and others were part of the Inverness, Scotland McIntosh clan that Oglethorpe recruited in 1735 to fight the Spanish in St. Augustine, ending in victory at the Battle of Bloody Marsh. The McIntosh Clan was on both sides of the Revolution with my own particular branch at the Siege of Savannah, albeit on the British side. I am also part of the old Mills cotton shipping family here whose forebear was scalped in 1818 in Fernandina with the family flee-ing to the safety of Savannah. The family was in the City when Sherman came with his army for a holiday visit at Christmas, 1864. So we've been around as they say.

The purpose in writing this book is that while there are many books on Savannah and its architecture, there are not many on what actually happened in and around these buildings and Squares. This book serves to fill that gap. You can read it before you go or carry it with you on your stroll and then read as you sit on a bench in one of the Squares. You should close your eyes in a mindfulness kind of way, listen to the sounds, picture the events being told, and then open your eyes seeing historical layers like fallen leaves softly laying on each other. Don't forget to stop to eat, drink and have some ice cream as well. I've tried hard not to ramble and get distracted, but occasionally I could not help myself.

Starting Out

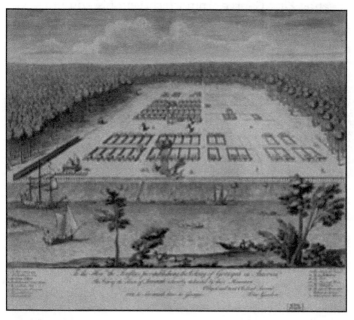

March 1734 engraving of Savannah, a year after Oglethorpe landed

Like Oglethorpe in 1733 I'd like to start out in front of City Hall which stands on the Strand, now known as Bay Street. When Oglethorpe chose the site near City Hall the bluff was 40 feet high and the water depth 12 feet near the bank. Also near the bank were fresh water springs underneath quick sand. The channel is 47 feet in its current state.

Oglethorpe pitched his first tent between Bull and Whitaker streets on Yamacraw Bluff. There is a bench marking his spot just to the west of City Hall in front of the Hyatt. He soon signed a treaty with the elderly Tomochichi, the chief of a scraggly band of Creek Indians called the Yamacraws. A year later he took Tomochichi to London meeting King George. Tomochichi and his entourage got to ride around in a carriage with 6 white horses and saw the changing of the guard conducted by the King himself!

The Indian's village was called Yamacraw and was near where the bridge over the Savannah River now enters the city. It is said the name comes from a branch of the Shawnee called the Sawannos or Savannahs that settled along the river. By 1725 most of them had moved north. In 1525 the Spanish explored up the coast all the way to Cape Fear in North Carolina. They found the Savannah River and named it Rio de la Cruz or River of the

Tomochichi and nephew

Cross. Later they called it Rio Dulce for Sweet River.

Oglethorpe and his group were the very last Europeans to settle in the area known as Georgia. Carolina traders had been crisscrossing the state for decades and even my ancestor "Tuscarora Jack" Barnwell came here to build Fort King George near Darien, a decade before Oglethorpe showed up. More than a 150 years before Oglethorpe started his colony, the Spanish had eliminated the French influence and established settlements both north and south of Savannah. The southern settlement near Darien was almost wiped out by the Guale Indian uprising in 1597.

It was to protect Charleston from the Spanish threat at St. Augustine that was the basis for the Crown allowing the Trustees to establish this 13th and last Colony in America. Indeed, the Spanish burned my family's house on Edisto Island in South Carolina in 1686. The foundation stones are still visible.

On the far eastern side of City Hall near the Trustees Garden or old Fort Wayne was a large Indian burial mound, which was later cut through to allow access to the other side. Human bones were found inside and there may still be some under the street. This area was known as Indian Hill later renamed in 1902 as Emmet Park for Irish patriot Robert Emmet who was executed by the British in 1803 for the exact same activity for which George Washington is honored. Washington was a successful revolutionary, Emmet less so.

Whenever I stand in front of City Hall I am reminded of one of my legal cases. The fellow was a postman and started to hear his radio talk to him personally. The radio told him to kill the Mayor. So he drove to the front of City Hall leaving the car running, pulled out a knife, and ran up to the second floor. The Mayor wasn't in so he left. Unfortunately he was arrested. But as a postman he had very good insurance and as his lawyer I promised that he would seek treatment, and the judge let him go with probation. This is how we did things in Savannah. Now he had other issues concerning a witch doctor in Blufton who swore she could put a romance charm on a red dress so his girlfriend would come back for the low, low price of $5000. How I got half his money back by negotiating with a certain New Jersey capo is a story for another day.

The front of City Hall is also the location where Gregory Peck in the original 1962 film *Cape Fear* with Robert Mitchum and Polly Bergen walked down the City Hall steps to the sidewalk and met evil Robert Mitchum for the first time. My mother, as the Mayor's wife, was in a photo op during the filming and told me he was very handsome. I think she had a crush. My mother wore white gloves. Polly Bergen did not. Polly Bergen also had on a pant suit, which was pretty risqué for Savannah in those days. Much later Burt Reynolds filmed scenes for *Gator* at City Hall.

City Hall was opened in 1906 on the site of an older building, the City Exchange, also used as a City Hall. The City Exchange was the entertainment locale when Aaron Burr, President Monroe, General Lafayette and other notables like them came to town. It was also the place in 1871 where 67 Georgian Confederate dead from Gettysburg were brought from that battlefield where they had lain for the last 8 years and lay in state before being buried at Laurel Grove Cemetery.

Around the time the new City Hall opened in 1906 my Great Aunt Cornelia Maclean designed the City's flag and received ten dollars in gold for it. Originally the building was to have classic Ben Hur type chariots on the roof as in Beaux-Arts style, but the expense caused them to be dropped. The result was a more slimmed down Italian Renaissance design. Above the front entrance is a portico where dignitaries (including me as a boy) would watch the St. Patrick's Day Parade march by.

As you walk inside the rotunda you can look up and see the stained glass dome above. It rises 70 feet and used to be clad in copper but was covered with gold in 1987. In front is the Cherub water fountain with a marble basin where I used to play with the large goldfish as a boy. They have since discontinued them. Goldfish were introduced in 1906 when the building was first opened. Immediately someone placed two small alligators in the basin. These have since been removed.

The City runs a tour once a month on the first Tuesday and if you are in town you should go. The Council Chamber on the second floor is a time capsule of how municipal buildings looked 100 years ago. It even used to have a large painting of Robert E. Lee in the Chamber as did many Southern cities of the period. In the Chamber are very large ship models which used to fascinate my younger self. The large 1916 model of the Steamship Savannah is now located at the Savannah History Museum. Along the stairs are pictures of the City's Mayors and as you travel up the stairs the pictures change marking the political transition from white men with fuzzy moustaches to women and African-Americans. You can even catch a picture of my father, although without any facial hair.

As you step out of City Hall take a small detour to the left and see the "Washington Guns," which naturally he never actually used. Instead he captured these light brass six-pounders at Yorktown and gave them to the Chatham Artillery, a local militia group when he visited

Savannah in 1791. One cannon is English and was cast in 1758 with the motto of the Order of the Garter. The other is French from the time of the Sun King, Louis XIV, and in Latin is engraved "Last Argument of Kings." They were taken back to Yorktown in 1881 and led the centennial parade. The guns were secretly buried during the Union occupation and resurrected in 1872 when occupation ended. At some point the Chatham Artillery named them "George" and "Martha," probably while drinking their famous potent punch. During a rehearsal in 1961 the Chatham Artillery fired off one of the 200 year old guns and blew off the breech.

Our sojourn begins on Bull Street which was named for Colonel Bull of Charleston who helped Oglethorpe lay out the streets and squares of Savannah. He had been a Captain in the Tuscarora War under my ancestor John "Tuscarora Jack" Barnwell. Mr. Whitaker of South Carolina gave the colony some cattle so he got a street and Mr. St. Julien helped out as well so he got one too.

As you walk down Bull Street to your immediate left is the formidable U.S. Custom House. It was completed in 1852 of granite from Quincy, Massachusetts and was designed by New York architect John Norris who also designed the Massie School and the Mercer-Wilder house, which tour guides now like to call the Mercer-Williams house. A widow by the name of Overend used to live in this location in a small house which Oglethorpe would rent when he came to town. He had to rent since although he founded the colony, he never owned any land.

In 1859 the famous slave smuggling case of the ship *Wanderer* was tried in this building some 50 years after the slave trade was legally abolished in 1808. The *Wanderer* had left New York flying the New York Yacht Club flag, sailed to the Congo and then smuggled 400 slaves into Jekyll Island, Georgia the year before. The government prosecuted the owners several times, but could never get a conviction. Northern newspapers were outraged. The case was the last of the infamous slave smuggling ship cases such as the *Antelope* and *Amistad*. The *Wanderer* eventually entered Union service during the War and was used for blockade duty.

Behind the Customs House is Bay Lane and where the lane approaches Drayton Street was where many of the dealers in slave auctions had their businesses. One of the largest dealers here was Joseph Bryan who handled the March, 1859 block sale of 429 men, women, and children owned by Pierce Butler from his plantations near Darien. Butler had gambling debts so he sold them. It rained for two days and the sale is called *"The Weeping Time"* as the rain mirrored the tears of the families that were broken up and sold. Butler's ex-wife was the famous Fanny Kemble, a British actress, who wrote a searing anti-slavery book called *Journal of a Residence on a Georgian Plantation in 1838-1839,* which is still in print. It was published in 1863 and may have influenced England's decision not to support the Confederacy.

The Hermitage

On your random walk you will hear of houses being made of Savannah grey brick. This brick today easily goes for 3-4 times the price of regular brick, if you can even find any. But back in the day it was what was used. It was made from special Savannah river mud at an up river plantation called the Hermitage. About 200 slaves worked at making these bricks. Even the slave cabins were made of brick. Fort Pulaski is made of millions of them.

In 1925 Henry Ford decided to keep up with his peer group of millionaires by buying the old Strathy Hall plantation on the Ogeechee River. My father's Great Aunt Eve was living there with her husband Robert Habersham Clay who owned it. The family story is that Ford offered twice the value during those times and they jumped at the price. Ten years later in 1935 Ford then bought the Hermitage, dismantled it, and used the bricks and pieces to build his own mansion at Strathy Hall. It has now become a high end residential development known as the Ford Plantation. He also dismantled two Hermitage slave cabins and shipped them to his Greenfield Village museum in Deerborn, Michigan where they are open to the public.

A photochrome image. On the left and right are the brick Hermitage slave cabins now in Detroit. At the end of the oak drive is the Hermitage before Henry Ford dismantled it.

The Hermitage before Henry Ford took it apart

Many downtown houses have high stoops with "English basements." Generally the kitchen was on this basement level. The living area was higher to get away from the sand, dust, noise, and bugs. Savannah streets for a hundred years were just ankle deep sand that not only made it difficult to walk, but also raised a lot of debris in the air. Having the parlor area higher also allowed cooling breezes to blow.

Johnson Square

As you walk to the end of the first block and view the building on the right on the southwest corner, this is where the famous Pulaski House Hotel was located. It was where everybody who was anybody stayed. It was built in 1835. General Sherman planned to stay there on the night of December 22, 1864, before Mr. Green breathlessly found him there and invited him to stay at his house on Madison Square, now called the Green-Meldrim house. Sherman had stayed at the Pulaski House before as a young lieutenant and was planning to do so again. In his memoirs Sherman recounts how the manager tried to charge him and how he replied that he was not in the habit of paying for his lodging, being that he was the leader of a conquering army of 62,000 men and all. Ironically, Mrs. Jefferson Davis also stayed there on her way back from visiting her husband in the prison at Fort Monroe, Virginia.

1906 photo of Johnson Square with the Pulaski House on the left with a horse and carriage at the entrance.

After Fort McAllister on the Ogeechee River was captured which allowed Sherman's army to finally be re-supplied from naval ships, he moved heavy guns in place to bombard the city. Sherman threatened to "make little effort to restrain his army." Like Tamerlane, Sherman had already proven he was not above pillaging as his army rampaged through Georgia.

On the night of December 20th, 1864, all cannons were spiked and Confederate troops quietly evacuated the city over pontoon boats into South Carolina. The evacuation began where Martin Luther King Blvd. meets the river and crossed to Hutchinson Island then to South Carolina. The current Highway 17 off the bridge into South Carolina parallels the route they took. Union Commanders suspected

*General Sherman reviewing troops on Bay
Street in front of the Customs House.*

they were leaving, but Sherman had ordered the troops
not to attack. After the troops left, civilian mobs began to
loot the city.

Union officers entered the empty trenches on the early
morning of the 21st at which time Mayor Richard Arnold
met with Union General Geary near the current Savannah
Visitors Center and surrendered the city. With desper-
ation and Armageddon in the air, looting mobs raged
throughout the city. Mayor Arnold asked for help and
General Geary established order by showing the mobs
the bayonet. Union troops paraded down Bay Street in
front of the Customs House that afternoon.

The troops tented in the squares. Prior to the surrender on December 21, 1864, Sherman ran aground on a mud bank off Wassaw Island on his way back from Hilton Head so was not actually present the day the City surrounded.

In truth while there certainly was some stealing and destruction of property in the city by the occupation army, Sherman did allow army rations to be distributed to the populace who would take them. Further, ships with food also arrived from Boston and New York. The occupation was a mixed blessing and while somewhat odd and peculiar to the inhabitants, it certainly could have been a lot worse. Indeed, the City later passed a Resolution thanking General Geary, the occupation commander, for helping maintain order in the city. To illustrate the change in some of the citizens, but by no means all, when ex-President Grant was touring the south in 1880 Savannah extended an invitation to visit and he accepted.

The manager of Pulaski House had a young daughter, Gracie. Just days after Easter in 1889 she died of pneumonia at the age of 6. Her parents commissioned a famous sculpture of Gracie, which is at Bonaventure.

Gracie; Photo by Leslie Alwiel

This 1835 hotel was demolished around 1956 and a Morrison's Cafeteria opened on the site. Regions Bank is now in this location. In the summer of 1963 Savannah experienced civil rights marches on Broughton Street seeking to integrate the lunch counters. One of the tactics was to send school children in to sit at this Morrison's. I'll let my father the Mayor describe it: "They would bring in a couple of thousand. It took a lot of doing to arrest them all. I mean it took all afternoon, and then you'd see them that night they'd be back on the street again. Nobody kept these kids in jail. They didn't need attorneys. The judges didn't keep them in jail. What are you going to do with all those little kids?" From Indians to Secession to Sherman to Civil Rights, this corner has seen it all.

The first square designed by Oglethorpe was Johnson Square named for the Royal Governor of South Carolina. The squares were established for general purposes such as markets and started out as just sand and dirt. In the middle of each square was a well and pump then after the Great Fire of 1820, a water cistern. Johnson Square is bordered by the streets Bryan and Saint Julien named for friends of the colony.

If you walk 5 blocks east to 507 East Saint Julien, you will come to the haunted Hampton Lillibridge House. It has had a Linda Blair type exorcism and everything. It also has an interesting widow's walk on top. I had doctor friends that used to live in it and they said doors would open and sounds could be heard. Something is just not right. Now the house has been moved from its original location and it is not unusual that houses that are moved are not level anymore so doors don't fit and window sills aren't tight allowing for drafts to swirl around. You decide. I could also tell you about the Lady in Red whose dress was dipped in the blood of her victims, but that just might be a story.

Now it was in Johnson Square that Oglethorpe had a major peace conference with both the Upper and Lower Creeks in 1735. Congress Street bordering the Square was originally called Duke street after the Duke of York, but was changed in 1803 as part of a plan to rename streets to eliminate royalist names. When you win, you get to rename your streets. It is more than ironic then to find that the Revolutionary Savannahians chose to keep the York street name next to Wright Square.

While the history is a little hazy there is evidence that after a Liberty Pole was raised by Savannah's Liberty Boys outside Tondee's Tavern another may have been raised in Johnson Square in early June, 1775. Georgia, being the youngest colony, felt more tied to Britain's apron strings than others and was slow in coming around in proclaiming its freedom. After Savannah received the news of Lexington's battle in April, 1775, all that changed. The Liberty Boys, whose members included the most prominent men, spiked and rolled 20 cannons off the bluff to the river. They then attacked the powder magazine on the eastern side of the bluff and stole away large amounts of powder. The story is that some of this powder made its way to Bunker Hill. The third reading of the Declaration of Independence in Savannah was in this Square.

Buried in the Square is Revolutionary War General Nathanael Greene. Washington sent General Greene to replace the disastrous Gates and Greene won the Revolutionary War when Cornwallis defeated him in a pyrrhic victory at Guilford Courthouse in North Carolina. Cornwallis lost so many soldiers that he was forced to retreat to Yorktown and enter historic ignominy. This allowed Greene to liberate South Carolina. To honor his service Georgia confiscated from its royalist owner and gave him Mulberry Grove Plantation up river from Savannah. The Greene monument is the second oldest obelisk in the country.

Mulberry Grove is where Eli Whitney, Greene's children's tutor, invented the cotton gin (with perhaps some unaccredited help from the vivacious Mrs. Greene) in 1793. A decade of fruitless patent litigation followed. Within 15 years cotton exports from the United States grew from 200,000 pounds to 64 million. Rice planting was still part of Savannah's economy, but took a back seat. Cotton was King. Whitney finally made some money when he moved back to Connecticut and endorsed the idea of producing interchangeable machine parts for muskets.

In the 1840's and 50's my Great Grandmother's family, the Mills, had several ships shipping cotton monthly from Savannah to Liverpool. This was one of their ships called the CONSUL, painted around 1852. Note that the waves seem to go in one direction and the sails in another. There is also a steamer in the background.

Mulberry Grove Plantation is now part of the Georgia Ports complex where large commercial container ships offload. Like Grove Point Plantation, the mansion was burned by Sherman for no particular reason and its jungle covered ruins and a handful of 300 year old oak trees are the only remaining vestiges. General Greene was originally buried at Colonial Cemetery, but Union soldiers badly vandalized the cemetery and his remains were lost. They were rediscovered and his bones placed in Johnson Square in 1901 along with his son who had drowned in the Savannah River.

The cornerstone of the Greene obelisk was laid by the Marquis de Lafayette when he visited Savannah in 1825 on his 5000 mile North American tour. Lafayette also laid the cornerstone for the Pulaski monument at the same time although that monument would not be constructed for another 30 years. Lafayette stayed at the Owens-Thomas house when he was here. Lafayette and Greene were very close and Greene's son who drowned had been taken to France by Lafayette to be educated. The obelisk is from the same quarry used in building the New York City Hall. In 1847 the famous Daniel Webster gave a rousing speech in front of the monument. It is said that even "Mr. Scratch" liked it. In digging the foundation workers found a tile on which the year 1782 was inscribed and part of a log. It was speculated that this marked the spot where the Liberty Pole was again raised after the British evacuated.

Below is a print of the wild scene in Johnson Square on November 8, 1860, upon hearing of Lincoln's election. While Lincoln did not run on an abolitionist ticket, Southern leaders were completely convinced that a man who held personal abolitionist views although not political ones was an overwhelming threat to them. Of course, Jefferson Davis as Secretary of War also thought it made sense to import camels to Texas. Lincoln wasn't even on the ballot in Georgia.

The first Flag of Independence raised in the South by the Citizens of Savannah, Ga. November 8th 1860.

A night time general meeting was held in the crowded Square calling for a state secession convention. A banner was placed on Greene's monument showing the image of a coiled rattlesnake with the words *"Our Motto Southern Rights, Equality of the States, Don't Tread on Me."* The scene was lit by fireworks and a bonfire. The old City Exchange building, later replaced by City Hall, is visible behind the monument with the Pulaski Hotel to the left. The wild scene foreshadowed the insanity of the next 4 years. Mr. Lincoln's War was caused by Secession and Secession was caused by slavery. Although Georgia was the last of the 13 colonies to allow slavery, eighty years after Massachusetts freed its slaves, Southern slavery, based on a greater economic incentive was still going strong.

In the ultimate irony, four and half years later on April 22, 1865, in this same spot, there was a mass meeting by five thousand people mourning Lincoln after his assassination. My Great Great Grandfather Mills was a member of the committee arranging this mournful gathering. Statements were printed on white bands tied from tree to tree around the Square such as "How are the Mighty Fallen," and "He died, but his work still lives."

Some Savannah business leaders had mixed feelings about Secession, although not slavery. They were simply making too much money as this Currier & Ives 1861 illustration indicates. The artist used the image of two parties, Governor Pickens of South Carolina and President Buchanan, pulling on the different ends of a cow, while a man in the middle (identified as "Georgia") happily milks the country into a bucket labeled Savannah.

My family, the Mills, was not enthusiastic about

Secession and took half their money and invested it in England. With the other half they bought Confederate bonds. It pays to play both sides sometimes. One of the three brothers spent 4 years touring Europe while the war raged before coming home.

Soon after Sherman's occupation Savannah held a large meeting saying they were now fine with being part of the Union. Imagine that! Augusta and other Confederate cities castigated Savannah for its cowardice, but within days Savannah was focused on getting back to business and that business was shipping "white gold" known as cotton. Savannah has always been a very practical city. Having tried secession and lost a war, the city was ready to move on.

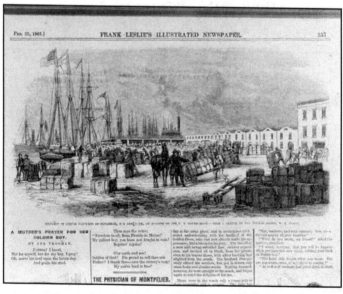

Cotton shipping out of Savannah in February, 1865

On the eastern side of Johnson Square is Christ Church built in classic Greek Revival style in 1838 on the site of the original Christ Church which burned in the great fire of 1796 that consumed half the buildings in the city. Christ Church was built on its original trust lot and has never moved. The church bell was made by Paul Revere's firm in 1819. The stained glass portrait of Jesus is by Tiffany. General Lafayette attended services here when he visited in 1825. Johnny Mercer, the great song writer (" *On the Atchison, Topeka and the Santa Fe, Moon River"*) and Judy Garland's lover was a choir boy here. They say the studio married her off when she was 19 to get her away from him. His statue is in Ellis Square. He once wrote of Savannah, "You gave me a childhood not many could know, And I blow you a kiss from the bald-head row."

John Wesley, founder of Methodism, served for a time in the original Christ Church. He and his brother had a very bizarre experience in Savannah and eventually hated the place so much that they went back to England where he had an epiphany and founded a new denomination. Savannah hated them too and was glad to see them go. He had a dalliance of sorts with a girl who later married another then refused to give her church rites. The town was outraged. He has a monument in Reynolds Square near where he used to live, but note he had to slip out of Savannah in the dead of night. Jefferson Davis attended Sunday services on his visit here in October, 1863.

After 1810 the Squares were lit with oil lamps. The oil was from whales, the price of which eventually reached over $1,000 a barrel by 1860. The Confederate raider *Shenandoah*, on which my mother's Grandfather was a lieutenant, put a stop to most of the whale killing in 1865 as did the simultaneous advent of refined oil from Pennsylvania. They had to fight in Russian waters with a mostly British and Hawaiian crew, but after burning 35 whaling ships, the whales, but not the Confederacy were saved!

As you walk toward the next Square you will cross over the original commercial street known as Broughton. It was named for the Lieutenant-Governor of South Carolina. In the middle of the intersection was a well, now paved over. Just as an aside, if you go left a block you will find Leopold's Ice Cream, a 100 year old ice cream parlor. Its current owner, Stratton Leopold, is descendant of the original owner and a Hollywood producer and his movies (*The General's Daughter, Sum of All Fears*) are represented by posters gracing the walls. The almost Oscar winning movie *SpongeBob SquarePants 2* was filmed on Broughton Street.

Wright Square

We now come upon Wright Square named for Georgia's last Royal Governor. It was originally called Percival Square for Lord Percival and was considered the center of town and where the public market was located. Somewhere to the west on York Street is a small cemetery now lost and paved over. They hung poor Alice Riley here in 1735 for murdering her master, William Wise, as she was his indentured servant. If you read between the lines and speculate a bit, he likely had it coming. He once took a woman of the town aboard his ship, but claimed she was his daughter. He was always causing trouble. In 1734 Alice and another servant, Richard White, strangled him with a necktie and drowned him while washing his hair. Some 9 months later she produced a child and then was hung. Who was the father you ask? You may continue to ask, but the dead tell no tales.

A few short years after Chief Tomochichi made it back from London he died in 1739 and was buried in this square with a pyramid of stones gathered over his grave. Oglethorpe was a pallbearer and the militia fired their guns in honor. In 1899 the Georgia Society of Colonial Dames placed a large boulder near where they thought he was buried to mark his grave. The story is that the 1884 Gordon Monument was actually built on top of

Tomochichi's grave and Gordon's daughter-in-law Nellie Gordon, mother of Juliette Gordon Low, was outraged and so led the effort to place a boulder from Stone Mountain honoring the Chief. The story continues that the monument company sent her a bill due on "Judgment Day" as they did not want her to pay anything. Instead she paid the bill saying that on Judgment Day she would be occupied with her own affairs!

The Gordon Monument is very interesting with Corinthian capitals supporting four winged figures holding a globe. The four figures represent agriculture, manufacturing, commerce and art, symbolizing prosperity. It honors the founder of the Central of Georgia Railroad that boosted commerce by connecting the port of Savannah to the hinterlands for the cotton trade. Gordon worked himself to death at a young age in building the railroad that eventually allowed Savannah to become a huge cotton export harbor.

Wright Square is surrounded by State, President and York streets. State Street used to be Prince Street and President was King, but in 1803 were renamed reflecting the Revolutionary War winners. Note that Charleston did not do the same. York Street was named for the Duke of York.

From the very beginning of the Colony until about 40 years ago the County Courthouse had always been located on this Square in the same location on the eastern side. The current Courthouse structure was built in 1889. The Courtroom was on the second floor and had a large ceiling fan similar to the courtroom scene in *To Kill a Mockingbird*.

The Courtroom's most famous trial was a 1970 contested will trial known as the Diamond case. It went up and down to and from the Georgia Supreme Court several times. The famous lawyer, Melvin Belli, from San Francisco made an appearance. Knowing I was bored during the summer, my father decided it was just the thing for me to attend as entertainment so dropped me off to watch. Mr. Belli brought his very California wife with him and at some point during the proceedings asked her to get his glasses. She got up off the spectator bench and sashayed through the swinging gates and bent over to hand them off. The trial stopped dead in its tracks. Every juror stared in her direction. Then she sashayed back. Savannah had never seen such theatre. As a 14 year old boy all I could do is quote Gomer Pyle and say to myself "Golly!"

It was in this Square that the Declaration of Independence was read on August 10, 1776, having just arrived from Philadelphia that morning. At the end of the reading President Bulloch of the Provincial Congress announced:

> And for the support of this Declaration,
> with a firm reliance upon Divine Providence,
> we mutually pledge our lives, our fortunes,
> and our sacred honor.

The Declaration was read out loud four times that day. Celebration ensued. Later in the evening, in front of the Courthouse, George III was interred in effigy. A burial service was read:

> For as much as George the Third, of Great Britain, hath most flagrantly violated his Coronation Oath ....we, therefore, commit his political existence to the ground

Unfortunately, in December 1778, the British captured the city and although the French under Count D'Estaing (including the future Haitian revolutionary Henri Christophe) and General Benjamin Lincoln attempted to retake the city, they failed. Savannah remained in British hands until the end of the war not leaving until July, 1782.

It was in front of the Courthouse that sales of slave men, women, and children occurred on the first Tuesday of the month.

On the western side of the Square is the federal courthouse. It was built in 1898 of Georgia marble on a granite base. Many years ago a certain very new federal judge decided to hold trial on St. Patrick's Day. Savannah tends to get about 250,000 boisterous visitors for the parade. I was part of the trial team when the noise level increased considerably. This very new federal Judge from out of town told the U.S. Marshals to go outside and tell the crowd to be quiet. The Marshals quietly took the Judge aside and explained to him that they were not going to do that. It was the last time he ever held trial the week of St. Patrick's Day.

The Lutheran Church is next to the old county courthouse and has a very nice stain glass picture of the ascension. A prior church building on the site served as a civil war field hospital. During the occupation Union soldiers used the pew cushions as pillows and burned the pews for firewood.

We now cross Oglethorpe Avenue, formerly known as South Broad Street. The name was changed in 1897. South Broad was the end of the original city plan. There was a palisade of wood around the whole town and two guard houses at an entrance on South Broad. The southern wall closely paralleled what is now Oglethorpe Avenue. The wall was necessary to protect against both Spanish invasion from St. Augustine and from any Indian attacks. Prior to building the wooden wall, painted planks were nailed to trees. White was painted on the north side showing the limits of the white man and red painted on the south to show all the rest was Indian land.

Previously Mary Musgrove, who had provided Oglethorpe with a lot of help, had changed personalities and become her evil twin Mary Bosomworth. As Mary Bosomworth she demanded excessive payment for her services and brought 200 Indians to town threatening to kill everyone if she didn't get her land. As you can imagine this concerned the citizens and this palisade wall was built. A marker honoring the good Mary Musgrove is in Lafayette Square. The bad witch version didn't get a marker.

I don't want you to get distracted, but east on Oglethorpe Street is the Old Cemetery now called Colonial Cemetery. It used to be larger than it is now and when Oglethorpe Street was widened it may have paved over some of the graves so drive quietly. About 10,000 people were buried in the Cemetery.

In the median of Oglethorpe Avenue near Bull Street is a marker for the old Jewish cemetery plot allocated by General Oglethorpe that was just outside the walls. They came on the second ship to Savannah and supposedly he let them stay when he received a legal opinion from some Charleston lawyer that only Catholics, but not Jews, were banned from the colony. In truth, he needed them and their doctor as Savannah had none and was undergoing an epidemic. Once Dr. Nunes was put to work the mortality rate dropped from 12% to 1%.

Juliette Gordon Low

Juliette Gordon Low's childhood home is on the corner of Bull and Oglethorpe and serves as the National Girl Scout Headquarters. The house was designed by the famous William Jay and built in 1818. The owner, Judge Wayne, later sold it to his niece Sarah Gordon. Wayne was a United States Supreme Court Justice for over 30 years. President Taft stayed with the Gordons at the house when he visited Savannah in November, 1909.

Juliette was only 5 when Sherman entered the city during Christmas, 1864. Her mother, a staunch Confederate, armed herself when she saw troops in front of the house. Juliette's mother's father and brothers were in the Union army so Sherman knew of the family and brought the children candy. He would visit them several times. General Carlin stayed at the house and had the army band play outside for the children's amusement. Juliette's father was in the Confederate Army and when she saw that General Howard was missing an arm said that she shouldn't wonder if her papa did it as he has shot lots of Yankees. Even at 5 years of age the founder of the Girl Scouts was a bit feisty.

Sherman and His Generals

Far left is Gen. Howard with one arm who little Juliette Gordon told that maybe her father had shot it off; Sherman seated in the center

I don't want to digress, but a block east of Juliette Low's house down Oglethorpe Avenue at 143 Abercorn Street near York Lane was the house where Shoeless Joe Jackson lived with his Savannah wife. Although he was acquitted in the infamous Black Sox Scandal he was still banned from baseball by baseball's first commissioner. He and his wife moved back to Savannah and lived here while running a dry cleaning establishment on State Street.

At 207 Bull Street is Independent Presbyterian Church built in 1817-19 from Quincy, Massachusetts granite and inspired by the Church of St. Martin-in-the-Fields in London. It was almost totally destroyed in the great 1889 fire then rebuilt exactly. Many of its stained glass windows were given by my great grandmother's family, the Mills. The marble baptism font is original to the church and survived the fire. President

Independent Presbyterian Church

Wilson was married next door to his Savannah bride, granddaughter of the pastor. She was his first wife and they had 3 daughters. The first daughter oddly enough became a Hindu nun. It has been said that the first wife was interested in the poor, but Wilson was an ardent racist. His second wife ran the country when Wilson stroked out.

Chippewa Square

Now we come upon Chippewa Square. It was established in 1815 to honor the Battle of Chippewa in the War of 1812. The Battle of Chippewa was fought in 1814 when the Americans, once again, invaded Canada. The young nation was successful and defeated the British on the field of battle.

Chippewa Square is bracketed by the streets Hull, McDonough and Perry. Hull Street is named for Commodore Isaac Hull, America's greatest Naval officer of the 1812 War. Hull was bred to be a sailor and found himself in command of the USS Constitution when he faced off against the HMS Guerriere. With his guns double shotted with round and grape he first fired when they were within pistol shot. Soon the enemy ship was a wreck. Some of Guerriere's rounds hit the USS Constitution and bounced back in the sea giving the ship its famous name of "Old Ironsides." The ship's hull was almost 2 feet thick and built of live oak and white oak from the swamps near St. Simons, Georgia. It is currently in Boston harbor and is still the oldest active ship in the United States Navy ready to defend us against the British at any time.

McDonough was another Great Lakes hero and as Commodore defeated the British on Lake Champlain in 1813 ending their invasion of the United States from Canada.

Perry was named for Commodore Oliver Hazard Perry to honor his victory at the Battle of Lake Erie on September 10, 1813, when he defeated the British. This is sometimes called the Battle of Put-in-Bay, but our history books can't handle that so they refer to the easier name. This victory allowed for the retaking of Detroit and forced Tecumseh to retreat after which he was killed in battle.

The square contains a statue of General James Oglethorpe facing south so as to defend the city from the Spanish. It is where Forest Gump sat as well. His bench is in the Savannah History Museum. Oglethorpe's statue was created by Daniel French, who also created the Lincoln statue inside the very strange Roman Imperial Lincoln Memorial in Washington. You have to admit the Lincoln Memorial is not in keeping with the American ideals of our founders and Lincoln was a rather humble person at that. French also created the famous Minute Man statue at Concord, Massachusetts.

On the left of the Square is the Savannah Theater. It may not look like it, but it was originally built in 1818 and designed by the famous architect John Jay. It is considered the oldest theater in America in continuous operation. Both Edwin Booth, John Wilkes Booth's brother, played *Hamlet* here. Oscar Wilde, Sarah Bernhardt, Lillian Russell and even the baseball star Ty Cobb were performers. Alexander Stephens who became Vice-President of the Confederacy gave a rousing speech in defense of secession in this theater. Later General Sherman attended a performance when he came to town with his 62,000 men. It has survived hurricanes and fire damage. After the last fire it was redesigned in Art Deco style.

Picture of how the theater used to look.

Across the square is the Philbrick-Eastman house at 17 West McDonough. It is a huge Greek Revival Mansion built in the 1840's. The Doric columns are incredible and so typical of a Cluskey designed house. Look for the medallions of famous men along its iron fence such as Lord Byron, George Washington and the English poet Robert Story. This same medallion design is on the fence in front of the Cotton Exchange on Factor's Walk. Both fences were taken from the famous Wetter house after it was unfortunately demolished in 1950.

The First Baptist Church is also located on this square. It is the oldest continuous house of worship in Savannah having opened in 1833. It is a perfect example of Greek Revival architecture and was the only church to perform services through the entire Civil War.

As you continue from Chippewa toward Liberty Street you will pass the unique Six Pence Pub. Julia Roberts once argued with her movie husband Dennis Quaid in front of it during filming of *Something to Talk About.*

Philbrick-Eastman house photo taken by Elisa Rolle

You might notice that some of the houses in this area have a cross or ship's wheel design cut into them about 20 feet off the ground. This is where a bolt was drilled through the entire house for stability after the powerful August 31, 1886, earthquake. It is estimated that the earthquake was a 7 on the scale. Both Charleston and Savannah felt considerable tremors and buildings were damaged. It was said that the buildings "shook like a wet dog." Many people slept outdoors in tents for days after. Allegedly the Waving Girl, Florence Martus, was mute and after the earthquake began to speak. I'm not so sure about that story. See if her statue on River Street speaks to you. You can see a lot of these bolts as you walk down Liberty Street from Bull. They are in the area near the top of the stairs to the row houses. If you do take the walk, very near Bull Street on Liberty is a great bookstore, "The Book Lady." Watch your step!

After crossing Liberty Street look to your left at the Desoto Hotel. It is a replacement for the old Desoto which had a large wrap around wooden porch with caned-backed rocking chairs. Nothing could be finer. The old Desoto hosted Presidents such as Taft, McKinley and Wilson. My Uncle and his friends were life guards at the hotel pool. Built in 1889 the old Desoto was deemed to be too difficult to restore and so was torn down and re-placed. The location was originally a military barracks during the Revolution and Civil War. Fierce fighting took place here when the British captured Savannah. George Walton, signer of the Declaration, was severely wounded while rallying the troops near here.

Madison Square

Now we come to Madison Square, named for the President who got our Capitol sacked and burned in 1814 by committing us to a war against the most powerful nation on Earth when we only had a small army and navy. Opposing Madison's War, New England entertained thoughts of seceding from the Union. So we honored him in 1839 with a Square.

1910 Picture of Sergeant Jasper with the old Desoto Hotel in background

The statue of Sergeant Jasper shows his truly heroic action of holding his hand over his fatal wound while never letting go the standard during the Revolution's 1779 Battle of the Siege of Savannah. His bullet riddled hat lies at his feet. Sergeant Jasper had also served with Francis Marion, the "Swamp Fox." This story may have been embellished by one of Parson Weems' fictions as he was also the author of Washington and the cherry tree, but I like the Sergeant so I will hold to his heroism.

The mortally wounded Jasper was carried back to his lines where he lay when Major Horry came upon him. " I have got my furlough said he, and pointing to his sword continued: That sword was presented to me by Governor Rutledge for my services in defense of Fort Moultrie. Give it to my father and tell him I have worn it with honor. If he should weep, say to him his son died in the hope of a better life... may the blessings of Providence rest upon my country and her cause."

Governor Rutledge of South Carolina is some sort of ancestor of mine and signed the Declaration of Independence. He was also known as "two bottle Rutledge" as he reportedly drank two bottles of Madeira every day. His brother John was nominated to the Supreme Court by Washington, but the Senate refused to confirm him. By all accounts they were typical South Carolinians who just did whatever they felt like and did not get along with any of the founding fathers.

A myth arose that Jasper was Irish and a militia group called the Irish Jasper Greens was formed in his honor. For those who like the truth, he came to Philadelphia in 1767 on a ship of immigrants from the German Palatinate and was likely brought over as an indentured servant. His name was anglicized by the ship's captain, who signed for him as he was illiterate. In 1876 Charles Colcock Jones, Jr. delivered a speech on Jasper saying "He sleeps with the brave dead of the siege who lie beneath the soil of Savannah." In a curious vein, it appears that General Sherman donated some money toward the monument. Notwithstanding his origins, he died fighting for freedom against the British and frankly what could be more Irish than that.

The monument was dedicated in 1888 in the Square before a crowd of ten thousand. President Cleveland made a brief appearance. A great time was had by all with huge fire works. No one sang the usual opposition's illegitimate child campaign ditty to Cleveland of "Ma, Ma where's my Pa; in the White House, ha, ha, ha."

This square is actually where the Americans had some of their defensive lines. In a dig in 2008 they actually found Revolutionary era musket balls near Jasper's statue.

My great grandmother's great grandfather was Rory McIntosh who was very blood thirsty always carrying around his claymore and also a bit of a nutter. He was inside the siege works fighting for the British. It was said that after the battle, a truce was arranged for the purpose of burying the dead, and several of the officers went out on the battle-ground, among them Rory, who strutted about, and said—"A glorious sight--our enemies slain in battle!" As I said, a nutter!

Facing Madison Square is the Green-Meldrim House. This is where General Sherman stayed while he was in the city. It is currently the Parish house for St John's Episcopal Church next door. The upstairs room is where Sherman conducted his business and where brides currently get dressed before their wedding. Charles Green was a poor Englishman who made his fortune in the cotton trade in the 1830's and 40's. Supposedly he lent the house to General Sherman in order to save his cotton, but Sherman confiscated it anyway. The house was later sold to Judge Peter Meldrim, a prominent Savannahian who was instrumental in getting Savannah State College off the ground. The house was built in 1856 and has Gothic elements throughout its design and in its iron work. I was once told that they used to light the candles in the high chandeliers to create a upward draft of air which cooled the house as a form of early air conditioning. Macon Street was closed off by my father to allow for safe passage from Church to Parish so if you use it, you can thank Dad.

At some point Secretary of War Edwin Stanton showed up to investigate claims that Sherman had mistreated the thousands of freed slaves that followed his army through Georgia. Stanton held a kangaroo court in the

Photochrom picture of Green-Meldrim House—Sherman's Headquarters

Green-Meldrim house and took testimony from African-American leaders. Sherman was acquitted. It was also here that Sherman learned of the death of his 6 month old son, Charles, whom he had never seen. His mourning was intense as his first son had also died.

St. John's Bishop was against secession and Union chaplains would give guest sermons to General Sherman and his officers from the pulpit. Other churches would ask Sherman if they could still pray for Jefferson Davis and he told them to go ahead as he needed it.

The streets Harris, Macon and Charlton bracket the Square. Harris was named after Charles Harris, a prominent lawyer and former Mayor of Savannah between 1802-04 who declined to serve as Judge when elected and also turned down becoming US Senator. My guess is he was just making too much money as a lawyer. Macon was named for a famous North Carolina Revolutionary War hero of whom it was said "never asked for public position for a relative." Since an honest politician is so rare, he deserved a street. The movie *The General's Daughter* with John Travolta was filmed in this Square.

Across the street from the Green-Meldrim house is a great independent bookstore, E. Shaver. It is in an 1842 building built by a female builder for her personal use and houses a terrific bookstore with a fine collection of books on Savannah. There is a nice pounce of cats as well. If you go to the Book Lady or Shaver's bookstore, pick up a copy of *Treasure Island*, as Captain Flint, whose treasure map Long John Silver was following died in Savannah of too much rum according to Robert Louis Stevenson. The Sherlock Holmes story of the *Adventure of the Speckled Band* also mentions Savannah.

Behind E. Shaver on Drayton Street is a dive bar called Pinkie Masters. In 1978 President Jimmy Carter stood on top of this bar during the St. Patrick's Day parade and gave a eulogy to its deceased owner. A plaque on the bar marks the spot.

Near Madison Square on Bull Street is the old Savannah Volunteer Guard Armory now restored by the Savannah College of Art and Design. It was built in 1892 on the site of the Savannah Female Orphan Asylum. The 24 pound cannons at the front were discovered underneath the old Armory when it was demolished. They may be of 1812 War vintage. The Guard participated in two famous horrific battles. The first was in defense of Battery Wagner in 1863 in Charleston and the other was in the last great battle of the Civil War at Sailor's Creek, Virginia on April 6, 1865. In this battle, just 3 days before Appomattox, 85 Guards took part and 30 were killed and 22 wounded, including my Great Grandfather, for total casualties of 61%.

Savannah has always exhibited public displays of martial support for whatever war we happen to be in at the moment. It was enthusiastic for the Spanish-American War for example. At the end of WWI a parade of Confederate Veterans marched by the Armory. Their sign read:

We Boys of -61
Extend Greetings to the Home Coming
Boys of 1917-1918 Who Entered the World War
Fought for Democracy and Gained the Victory

Across the street from the Armory/SCAD building is 341 Bull St. It is the home of the Masonic Lodge. Savannah founded the second oldest freemason lodge in the country in 1734. This building was started in 1913 and finished in 1923. A classical pilaster extends from the upper floors. It has many freemason motifs on the building such as the lion above the front door. Many buildings in Savannah have the same. Modern freemasonry dates back to England in the 1700's as a society promoting the enlightenment ideals of fraternity and equality. It is no surprise then that many of the Founding Fathers were freemasons.

In the corner of this building at 337 Bull is the current Gryphon Tea Room. This was the old Solomon's Pharmacy located here from 1913 until 1981 and you can see apothecary items inside. The original Solomon opened his first shop in 1845. They filled a prescription for General Robert E. Lee in 1870 when he was visiting. That pre-scription used to be dis-played in this store. Lee

Postcard of the Masonic Temple from SCAD postcard collection

came in the spring of 1870 on his way to visit the grave of his Revolutionary War hero father "Light Horse" Harry Lee who died on Cumberland Island. Lee would die in October, 1870. The pharmacy was a drug store, soda fountain and ice cream parlor. It was one of the oldest drug stores in the country until it closed.

Savannah's own gryphon or griffin is actually not a

gryphon at all, since it doesn't have an eagle's head, but is a 1889 red terra cotta winged lion in front of the Cotton Exchange on Factor's Walk off of Bay. If someone tells you it is a gryphon, just nod your head pleasantly. The wrought iron fence surrounding the winged lion is from the demolished Wetter house. Other pieces of this wonderful fence with its medallions of famous people surround the Philbrick-Eastman house on Chippewa Square.

Monterey Square

Finally we come to the last Square before Forsyth Park. This is the confusing Monterey Square. There were two similarly named battles during the Mexican-American War both occurring in 1846. There was the American victory in 1846 at the Battle of Monterey where the flagship of the American Pacific Fleet, *USS Savannah*, sailed into Monterey Bay and captured the city without a shot. Then in the same year on May 24, 1846, was the bloody Battle of Monterrey, different spelling, which ended in a stalemate and truce, so naturally we called it a victory. At this second battle the Savannah Scotch-Irish militia unit, the Jasper Greens, was involved. This unit's biggest fight in this war may have been with the Georgia Kennesaw Rangers who continued to harass them for their ethnic origins leading to a brawl. The Square may have been named to memorialize the second battle and the Jasper Greens, but the City spelled it after the first battle by mistake.

In the middle of the Square is a monument honoring Casimir Pulaski, a Polish adventurer, who was killed by grapeshot leading the French and American cavalry during the Siege of Savannah in October 1779. He was shot not far from his monument. The Georgia Historical Society claims to have the grapeshot that killed him. Some said he was buried at sea and others at Greenwich Plantation next to Bonaventure. There is stronger evidence for a sea burial.

He is sometimes referred to as "Count Pulaski" although he was never a real Count nor did he refer to himself as such. In 1854 when the monument was constructed, some bones were placed under the monument, but there have always been doubts about who was buried there. In 1996 the bones were dug up and found to be female, but with certain features similar to Pulaski. In 2019 using mitochondria testing and after several failures it was announced that the bones were indeed related to Pulaski's grandniece and concluded it was Pulaski under his own monument. To explain why his bones were female, the Smithsonian also declared that perhaps Casimir was on a gender journey and was intersex. I don't think the British cared when they shot him. Many people are not entirely convinced that the Smithsonian's "Miss Cassie Pulaski" findings were not based on something other than science as the historical record for a sea burial is strong. There has also been no replication of the mtDNA findings as of this date.

When he first arrived in America, Pulaski wrote to General Washington saying ``I came here, where freedom is being defended, to serve it, and to live or die for it." His English was very poor and there was much friction in his American cavalry command over his tactics which only seemed to consist of riding at the front of a charge. However, in the Battle of Brandywine in 1777 he led a charge that may have saved Washington's life. Subsequently, Washington made him a Brigadier General. Not wasting any time, in 2009 Congress proclaimed him an honorary Citizen.

On the east side of the Square is the Gothic synagogue Mickve Israel built in 1878. The congregation was founded not long after the colony by Spanish-Portuguese Jews and is considered to be the oldest Reform Judaism congregation in America. The émigrés sort of snookered the Trustees by coming unannounced and the Trustees told Oglethorpe to make them leave, but to his credit he welcomed them. One of the reasons was there was a doctor among them who helped the colonists overcome a bout of fever. The colony's only other doctor had died. The other reason was he received a legal opinion from some lawyer in Charleston stating that only Catholics, but not Jews, were banned from the Colony. The first boy born in the colony came from these Jewish settlers and his descendants are still living in Savannah today.

The congregation unanimously supported the Revolution and in 1789 President Washington wrote them a very nice letter, which they still have. The original 16th century Torah scroll brought from Portugal is kept in the synagogue. The story goes that allegedly the reason the building is in the shape of a cross is that to save an architect's fee they used the old plans for a church.

Illustrating that Savannah never wastes a good building, Mickve Israel once had a break away group called Bnai Brith Jacob Synagogue. They built their 1909 synagogue on Montgomery Street in a Moorish revival style similar to the 1870 Central Synagogue in New York City. Around 1970 an Episcopal church bought it. The building has twin towers so on one tower is the Star of David and on the other a cross. Inside, stained glass depicts scenes from the life of Jesus while above the front door are scenes from Judaism. The building is now owned by Savannah College of Art and Design.

Facing Monterey Square is the Mercer-Wilder House now sometimes called the Mercer-Williams. The house was originally designed for Confederate General Hugh Mercer, great grandfather of Johnny Mercer, but it was not completed before the Civil War broke out. After the war he sold the property to John Wilder. It is a good example of the Italianate Style that architect John Norris favored. It has a beautiful center staircase. General Mercer was a West Point graduate and classmate of Robert E. Lee. He had served as an aide to General Winfield Scott.

Mercer-Wilder House

At some point in the late 1960's Jim Williams bought it. Jim was from up-country as we say, but to his credit built a very fine antiques business. I did not run with his crowd as he was much older than I, but some of my friends did. He liked younger men. He would occasionally sell my mother some piece of over priced furniture and that made them both happy. My mother and father were invited to his first Christmas party and my friends to the second. I do recommend John Berendt's book *Midnight In the Garden of Good and Evil* as it is a great read. He tells the stories we all know, but he weaves them well. Since fiction and truth are closely intertwined, Clint Eastwood's movie of the book was filmed here as well.

In the Square they also filmed the movie *Glory* about the Civil War African-American 54th Massachusetts Regiment as it prepared to travel to Morris Island near Charleston and attack Battery Wagner. A large bronze plaque about them is on the Boston Commons opposite Beacon Street on which they marched at their departure. My great grandfather was with the Savannah Volunteer Guard defending the Battery, but fortunately his battalion had been relieved the evening before the attack. The 54th charged over the sands in a frontal assault, reached the ramparts and was slaughtered. The survivors were briefly part of the occupation force when the Union took the city.

The story about Jim hanging the Nazi flag outside across from Mickve Israel is absolutely true. In the Square they were filming a movie and the story is that Jim got miffed when the movie crew laid down dirt over the street around the square without asking him first so retaliated with the flag. That should give you a little insight into the sort of fellow he was. Big on ego, small on empathy.

After he killed Hansford he was out on bail and had the usual Christmas party and my father was taken to the back by his lawyer and shown a bullet hole in the floor. Several of my friends prosecuted him over the years and he was always found guilty until on the 4th trial when they moved it to Augusta and he was acquitted. Soon after that he passed away. It was always my opinion that if he had just pled guilty to manslaughter or some lesser offense, said he was sorry and wouldn't do it again, he would have been out in a year or so and back in business. Savannah used to be fairly lenient and understanding believing that sometimes these sorts of things just happen, but you do have to say you're sorry. Jim never could.

Next door at 7 West Gordon Street is my old law partner's house that was featured in the great show *This Old House.* You might be able to find it in some old episodes.

On the other side is 423-425 Bull Street which are twin houses built around 1850. It is said that a copy of these is also in New York City.

On the western corner of Bull and Gaston is the magnificent Italian Renaissance Armstrong House built in 1919. It was the last of the great houses. It later became the location for a college, then a law firm and has now been lovingly restored back to a residence. It shows up in the original 1962 *Cape Fear* movie with Gregory Peck. Mr. Armstrong was an executive of a shipping firm and had a bookkeeper by the name of Deutsch. Deutsch later became a slum

1919 picture of The Armstrong House

lord and was worth millions and then died without a will. I entered the legal fight over his non-existing will and found out he had spent his last years sleeping in a lawn chair, eating over a sterno, typing a history of Casimir Pulaski on a plywood table. I sometimes think it's the weather, but Savannah has had its share of Flannery O'Connor eccentrics. It only makes sense since she used to live here!

Across the street from the Armstrong House at the eastern corner of Bull and Gaston Streets facing Forsyth Park is the Molyneux house built for the British Consul in 1857. My family had business dealings with him during the 1840's. One-armed General Howard occupied this house during the Union occupation. His staff indulged themselves with the liquor supply of Molyneux and wrecked his library. During the Union occupation the interior of the house suffered great damage and the family presented the United States with a damage bill for $11,000, which is still unpaid. After the War, Confederate General Henry Jackson bought it. Jackson had been the US prosecutor against the owners of the slave smuggler ship *Wanderer*. It later became a private eating club called The Oglethorpe Club.

The senior law partner in our firm, Colonel Hunter, was a member of this club. While serving in the China-Burma-India Theater, he once shot a tiger which he used as a cover for his bed. He was an interesting fellow with a handle bar moustache. His brother was an ace in WWI. He once was working for a bank trying to collect some money from a bank client. He came out of the club and spied the debtor's car parked in front. He got a chain out of his car and tied it to the fire hydrant, which is still there, and wrapped it around the axle of the other man's car. The bank got their money after this fine piece of lawyering was done.

Candler Oak

Before entering Forsyth Park please detour down Gaston Street to Drayton and see the 300 year old Candler Oak. It is magnificent. Said to have begun around 1718, it has survived everything. A hospital was built next to it in 1791 and there was one at this location for the next 150 years or so. The hospital saw many yellow fever victims who were supposedly dragged out through tunnels under Drayton Street to be buried in Forsyth Park. The grand oak stood watch through it all. Both my Great Grandmother's father and her brother were Presidents of the hospital in the 1880's.

Yellow fever is not the same as malaria as yellow fever is caused by a virus carried by one kind of mosquito and malaria is a parasite carried by another kind. Yellow fever was the epidemic scourge of Savannah (1820, 1854, 1876) killing up to a 1000 inhabitants each time and emptying the city of all, but the dead. Noxious vapors called *miasma* from nearby rice plantations were believed to be the cause. While there is evidence that Africans with sickle cell trait have some immunity to malaria, there is no immunity to yellow fever. It struck both Savannah populations with deadly force.

The tree was in bad shape by the 1980's, but Savannah rallied around it and created the first conservation easement on a single tree in the nation. It is now lovingly cared for and should last another century.

The hospital by the grand oak was used by both the Confederacy and the Union for their soldiers. In 1864 imprisoned Union officers were moved from a bad Macon prison to a stockade by this tree. They immediately started to build tunnels to escape. One tunnel failed when a cow fell in it and could not get out. The officers only stayed six weeks before moving on, but soon in the fall of 1864 over seven thousand Union prisoners showed up having been evacuated from notorious Andersonville prison, victims of Lincoln's misguided policy against prisoner exchanges. They were placed across the park on the other side by Hall Street. These prisoners were so wretched that 500 Savannah women showed up with baskets of food to hand out.

Forsyth Park

We end this walking tour at Forsyth Park named for a pre-Civil War Governor and Senator from Georgia. The Park ends the development of the squares concept and was laid out in 1851. In the 1880s cows were still grazing in the Park Extension, beyond the fountain area. The beautiful fountain was built in 1858 and may have been inspired by the one in Paris' Place de la Concorde. Ironically, a duplicate of the fountain was later built in Poughkeepsie, New York to honor Union soldiers. The half man-half sea serpents spouting water are called tritons. To raise money for a fountain restoration bricks were sold and you can see the names of old Savannah families on these around the fountain. Even Tomochichi bought a brick!

Burt Reynolds performed a car chase around the fountain in *The Longest Yard.* You can see it in an Internet video. He also shot the cerebral film *Gator* in Savannah as well. Not to be outdone, Zac Efron rode a motorcycle around the fountain in the art film *Baywatch*.

On St. Patrick's Day, which is a really, really big deal in Savannah they dye the fountain water green. My father tried to dye the Savannah River green using fire tug boats, but winds picked up and the effort failed. Go big or go home.

The southern end of the park was used as a military parade ground. The Georgia Hussars used to play polo there. The dummy fort on the eastern side near Drayton Street was used for practice during WW1 training. Apparently they had never heard of trench warfare.

At the entrance to the Park were two Sphinxes. These were later removed.

The dog stayed.

The Park served as a tent ground for some thousands in the US Army headed to Cuba during the Spanish-American War. A statue honoring these volunteers is at the southern end of the Park. In December 1898 President McKinley and certain ex-Confederate officers who were now leading the army to Cuba reviewed a parade of 12,000 in the Park. Confederate General "Fighting" Joe Wheeler led one group of volunteers to Cuba and reportedly became confused during a skirmish yelling out "Let's go boys! We've got the damn Yankees on the run again!"

I hope you have enjoyed this little bit of history and the random walk. Now go have some ice cream! You've earned it.

About the Author

John H. Maclean has been a lawyer, Judge and author, but always in love with history. His family has been in Savannah since 1735 and in South Carolina since 1685.

Printed in the USA
CPSIA information can be obtained
at www.ICGtesting.com
JSHW011923150324
59196JS00001B/3